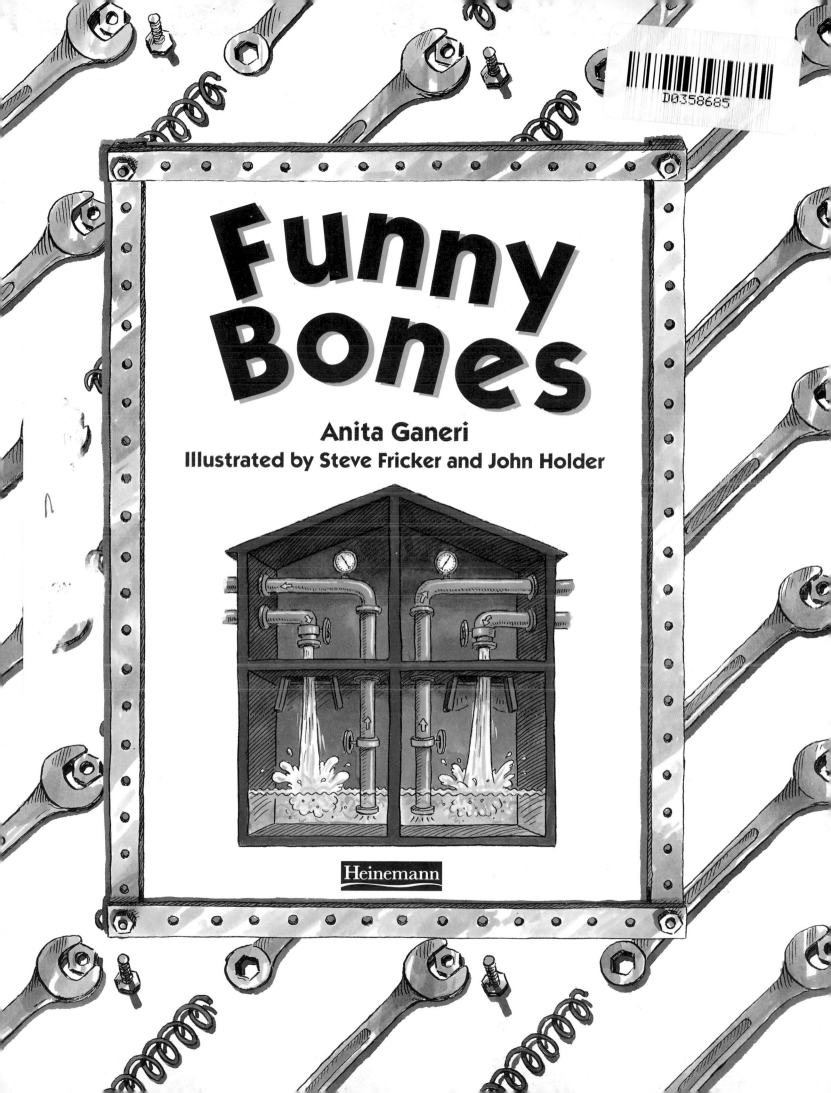

Funny Bones

Anita Ganeri

Illustrated by Steve Fricker and John Holder

Heinemann

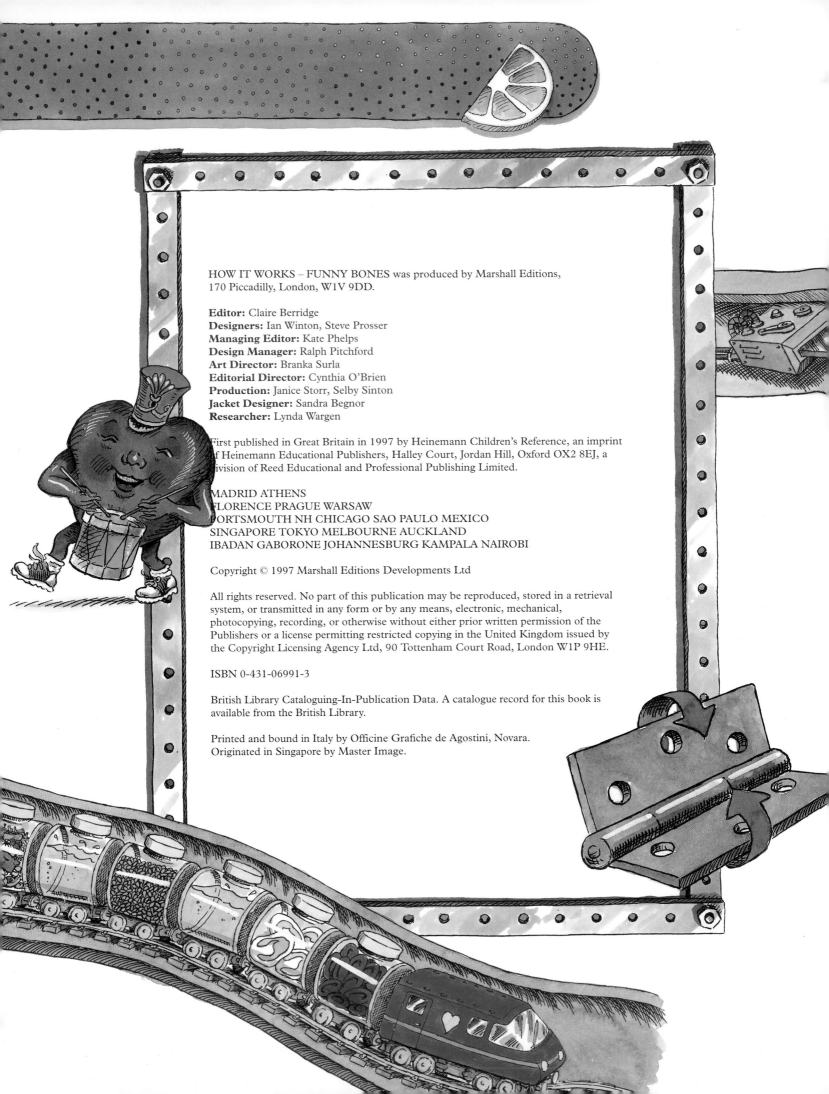

HOW IT WORKS – FUNNY BONES was produced by Marshall Editions,
170 Piccadilly, London, W1V 9DD.

Editor: Claire Berridge
Designers: Ian Winton, Steve Prosser
Managing Editor: Kate Phelps
Design Manager: Ralph Pitchford
Art Director: Branka Surla
Editorial Director: Cynthia O'Brien
Production: Janice Storr, Selby Sinton
Jacket Designer: Sandra Begnor
Researcher: Lynda Wargen

First published in Great Britain in 1997 by Heinemann Children's Reference, an imprint
of Heinemann Educational Publishers, Halley Court, Jordan Hill, Oxford OX2 8EJ, a
division of Reed Educational and Professional Publishing Limited.

MADRID ATHENS
FLORENCE PRAGUE WARSAW
PORTSMOUTH NH CHICAGO SAO PAULO MEXICO
SINGAPORE TOKYO MELBOURNE AUCKLAND
IBADAN GABORONE JOHANNESBURG KAMPALA NAIROBI

Copyright © 1997 Marshall Editions Developments Ltd

ISBN 0-431-06991-3

British Library Cataloguing-In-Publication Data. A catalogue record for this book is
available from the British Library.

Printed and bound in Italy by Officine Grafiche de Agostini, Novara.
Originated in Singapore by Master Image.

CONTENTS

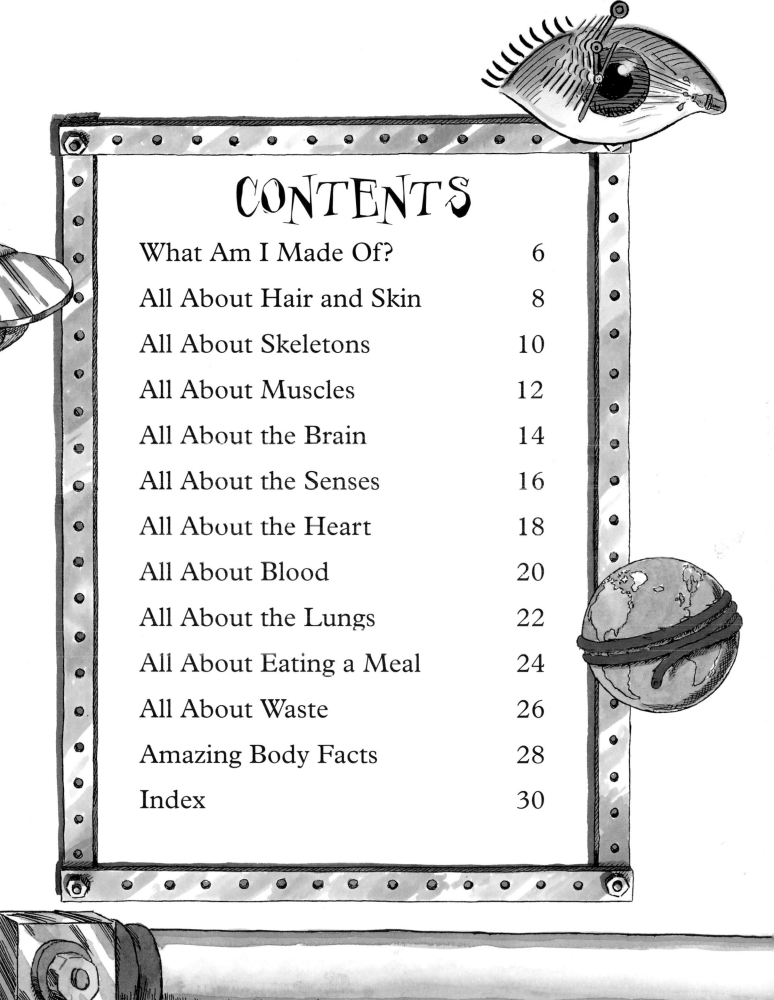

What Am I Made Of?	6
All About Hair and Skin	8
All About Skeletons	10
All About Muscles	12
All About the Brain	14
All About the Senses	16
All About the Heart	18
All About Blood	20
All About the Lungs	22
All About Eating a Meal	24
All About Waste	26
Amazing Body Facts	28
Index	30

Your body is truly amazing! Have a look in the mirror. What can you see? Eyes, hair, fingers, toes . . . And that's just on the outside. There are lots more body bits inside you, all working together like a well-oiled machine to keep you alive. Each of these bits is made of cells. On their own, most cells are too tiny to see. But put them together, and you've got you!

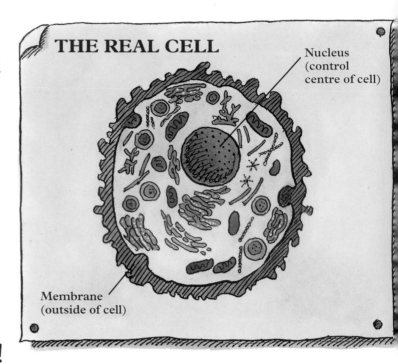

THE REAL CELL

Nucleus (control centre of cell)

Membrane (outside of cell)

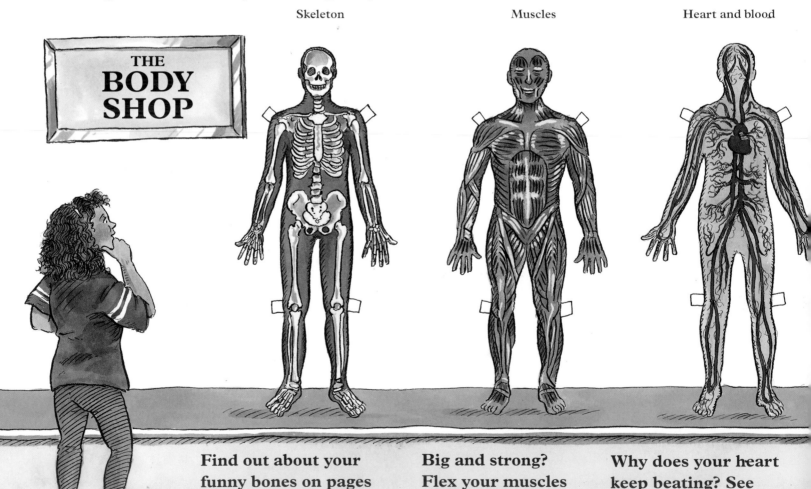

THE BODY SHOP

Skeleton

Muscles

Heart and blood

Find out about your funny bones on pages 10–11.

Big and strong? Flex your muscles on pages 12–13.

Why does your heart keep beating? See pages 18–21.

BODY BUILDERS

Cells are the building blocks of your body. There are millions and millions of them, with different jobs to do. Some make your blood, bones and skin. Others make your brain, muscles and nerves. Cells can split into two to make new ones which help you grow.

BODY BITS RECIPE
206 bones
640 muscles
9 pints of blood
All-over skin
5 million hairs
10 toenails
10 fingernails
2 eyes
2 ears
1 nose
32 teeth
ORGANS – 1 heart; 1 liver;
1 stomach; 2 lungs;
2 kidneys; 1 brain;
1 bladder; intestines (large and small)

Brain and nerves   Lungs and breathing   Food and digestion   Waste system

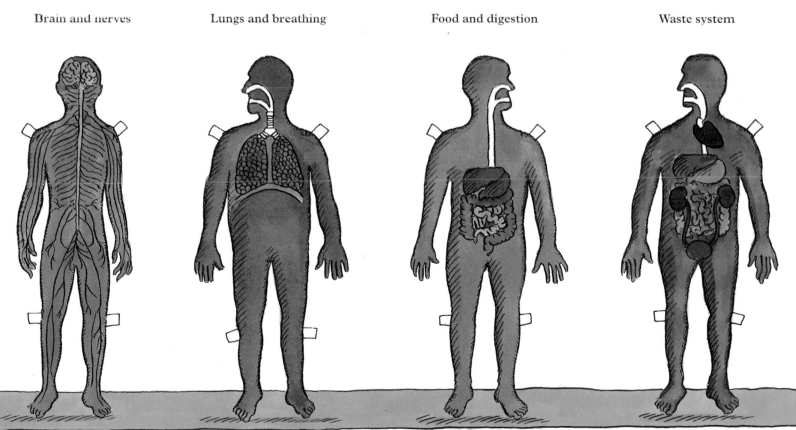

Read all about your amazing brain on pages 14–15.

Breathe in. . . Learn about lungs on pages 22–23.

Where does your food go? Find out on pages 24–25.

What about the bits you don't need? See pages 26–27.

ALL ABOUT HAIR AND SKIN

Your whole body is covered in stretchy skin. It holds all your body bits firmly together, and protects your insides from harm. It helps you to touch and feel things. And it can mend itself if you cut it. That's not all! Growing out of your skin are your hair and nails. Hair keeps your head warm in the cold and keeps the sun off it. And nails are useful if you've got an itch . . .

Like a diver's wet suit, skin is hard-wearing and waterproof. But it also lets you sweat on a hot day to cool you down. Phew!

Your skin makes oil to keep it soft and supple. Otherwise it would go wrinkly, like it does in the bath.

Skin is made of cells that overlap like tiny roof tiles.

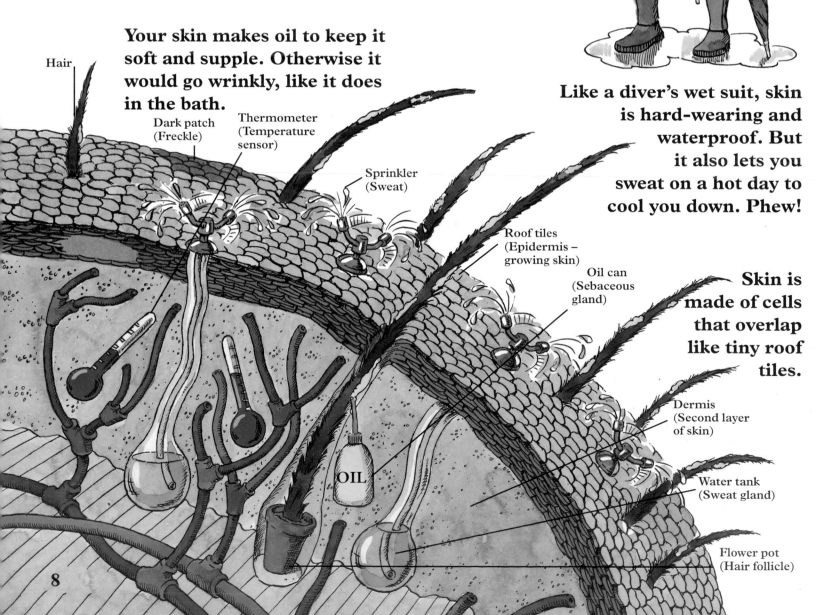

Hair

Dark patch (Freckle)

Thermometer (Temperature sensor)

Sprinkler (Sweat)

Roof tiles (Epidermis – growing skin)

Oil can (Sebaceous gland)

Dermis (Second layer of skin)

Water tank (Sweat gland)

OIL

Flower pot (Hair follicle)

HAIR STYLES
About five million hairs grow on your body. About 100,000 of these are on the top of your head.

Hair grows out of tiny pits in your skin. These are called follicles. The type of hair you've got depends on the shape of your follicles.

Wavy hair grows from oval follicles. Straight hair grows from round follicles. Curly hair grows from flat follicles.

REAL HAIR AND SKIN
Skin is made of two layers. The upper layer is the epidermis, the lower the dermis. The outside of the epidermis is made of dead skin cells. As these wear out new cells from the bottom of the epidermis replace them. Your hair and nails are also made of dead cells. That's why it doesn't hurt when you cut them.

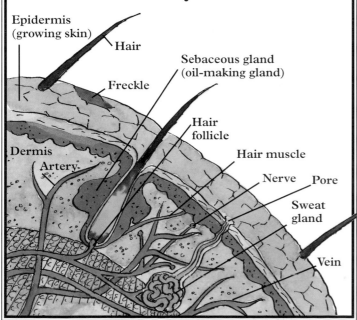

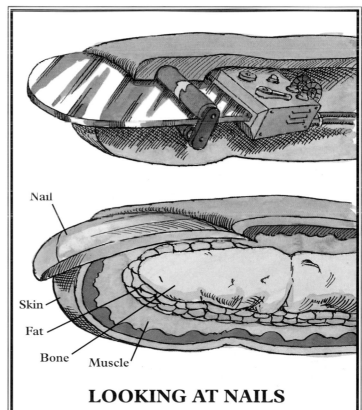

LOOKING AT NAILS
Nails are hard and tough to protect your fingertips. They grow from nail roots under the skin. Your fingernails grow faster than your toenails. And all your nails grow faster in summer than in winter!

9

ALL ABOUT SKELETONS

Without a skeleton, you'd flop to the ground in a jelly-like heap. Your skeleton holds your body up. It also protects the soft bits inside you. And it works with your muscles so you can move. Your skeleton is made of bones. They're solid and tough on the outside but hard and spongy underneath. They are also very light.

Crash-helmet (Skull)

Armour jacket (Rib cage)

Your skull protects your brain, like a bony crash helmet. Your rib cage is like a tough armour jacket around your heart and lungs.

The bones at a joint are held in place by ligaments, which are like elastic bands.

Hinge (Joint)

Elastic band (Ligament)

The bump in the end of your nose isn't a bone. It's squashy gristle. You can't see it on an X-ray because only your hard bones show up.

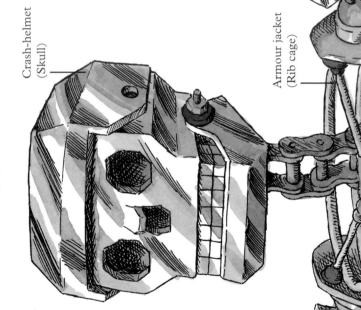

A REAL SKELETON

- Skull
- Breast bone (part of rib cage)
- Rib
- Back bones
- Hip bone (part of pelvis)
- Leg bones
- Knee cap
- Shoulder bone
- Arm bones
- Hand and finger bones
- Foot and toe bones

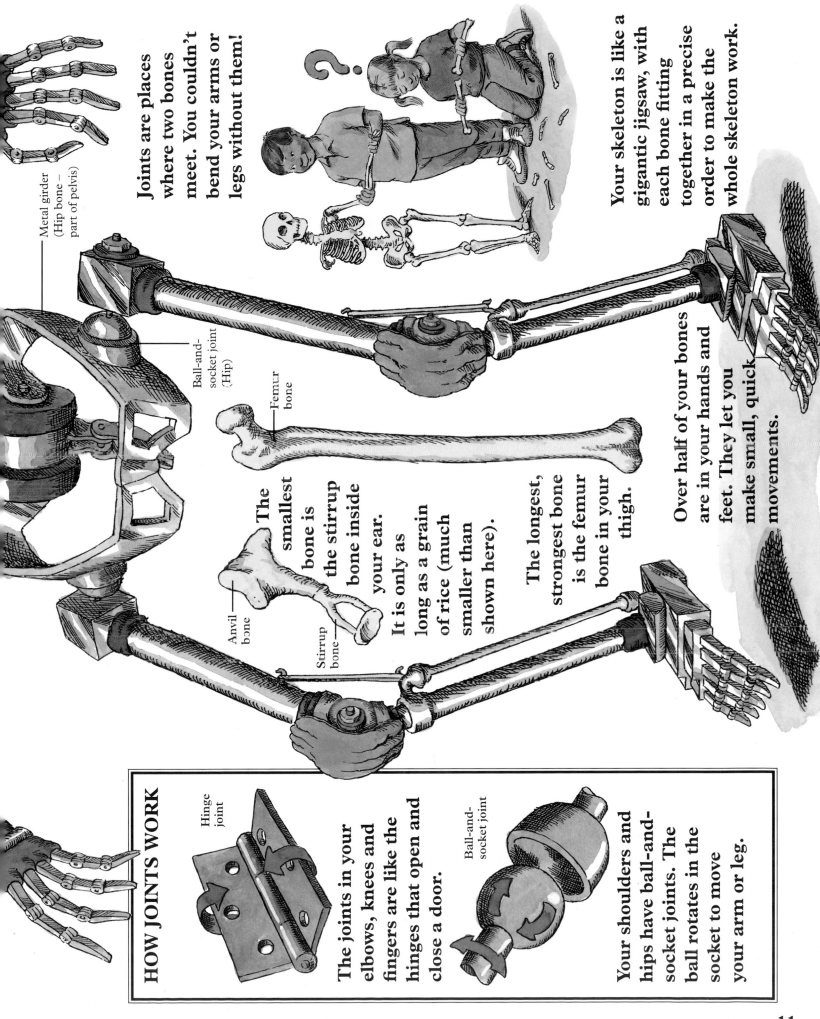

Metal girder
(Hip bone –
part of pelvis)

Joints are places
where two bones
meet. You couldn't
bend your arms or
legs without them!

Your skeleton is like a
gigantic jigsaw, with
each bone fitting
together in a precise
order to make the
whole skeleton work.

Ball-and-
socket joint
(Hip)

Femur
bone

The
smallest
bone is
the stirrup
bone inside
your ear.

It is only as
long as a grain
of rice (much
smaller than
shown here).

The longest,
strongest bone
is the femur
bone in your
thigh.

Over half of your bones
are in your hands and
feet. They let you
make small, quick
movements.

Anvil
bone

Stirrup
bone

HOW JOINTS WORK

Hinge
joint

The joints in your
elbows, knees and
fingers are like the
hinges that open and
close a door.

Ball-and-
socket joint

Your shoulders and
hips have ball-and-
socket joints. The
ball rotates in the
socket to move
your arm or leg.

ALL ABOUT MUSCLES

You might not be as strong as a weightlifter but you've got just as many muscles! Some are attached to bones. They work a bit like springs, pulling on your bones to make you move. Other muscles work your heart and lungs, and help you digest food.

To straighten your arm, the biceps muscle relaxes while the triceps pulls.

The brain controls all muscles, but some, like the heart, work automatically. This means you don't ever have to think about making it beat.

Spring
(Biceps muscle)

Many muscles work in pairs. To bend your elbow, the biceps in your arm pulls while the triceps relaxes.

The busiest muscles are in your eyelids. They make you blink about 20,000 times a day to wipe dust and grit from your eyes.

Spring
(Triceps muscle)

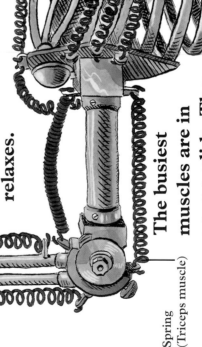

Facial muscles

Biceps

Stomach muscles

Bottom muscles (gluteus maximus)

Triceps

Chest muscles

Leg muscles (quadriceps)

Calf muscles

There are about 640 muscles all over your body, under your skin. They are made of bundles of tiny, thin fibres, like stretchy elastic threads. Each of these fibres is made of even finer threads. The whole muscle is covered with a stretchy layer to keep it in shape.

Your muscles are fixed to your bones by stretchy bands, called tendons. The longest and strongest tendon is the Achilles tendon between your calf and your heel. Try pressing it gently. It feels hard, like a bone.

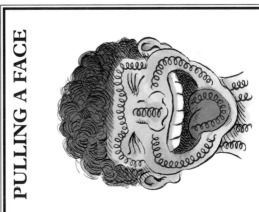

A third of your body weight is made up of muscle. Your biggest muscles are in your bottom! The smallest muscles are deep inside your ears.

Muscles need lots of energy to make them work. They get this from oxygen in the air you breathe and from the food you eat. Your blood carries the oxygen and food to your muscles.

PULLING A FACE

To pull a face as ugly as this one, you use about 30 muscles! These don't pull on bones, like the muscles in your arms. They pull on your skin instead.

Ouch!

Your brain is the most amazing machine! It's like a computer inside your head. Every bit of your body is controlled by your brain. It makes you move, think, feel and remember. Your body sends information to your brain. The messages whizz back and forth down long, thin wires called nerves, which run all over your body. Your brilliant brain sorts out this information and then sends a message back to tell your body what to do.

When you stub your toe, nerve signals race from your foot to other nerves that make your muscles pull your foot away. Your brain then sends you a pain signal.

SPEEDY NERVES

Nerves carry messages to and from your brain, in the form of electrical signals. Some whizz along at very high speed, even faster than a racing car. A thick bundle of nerves runs down your back, inside your spine. This is the main roadway between your body and brain.

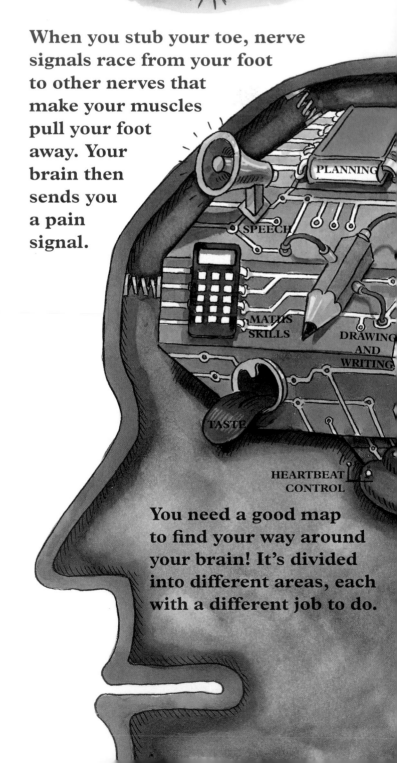

PLANNING

SPEECH

MATHS SKILLS

DRAWING AND WRITING

TASTE

HEARTBEAT CONTROL

You need a good map to find your way around your brain! It's divided into different areas, each with a different job to do.

It does not matter how big or small your brain is, size makes no difference to how clever you are! An adult's brain weighs about one and a half kilograms. It looks like a lump of soft grey blancmange.

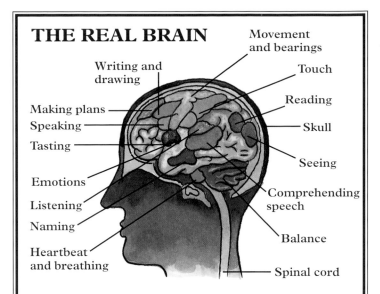

THE REAL BRAIN

Movement and bearings
Writing and drawing
Touch
Making plans
Reading
Speaking
Skull
Tasting
Seeing
Emotions
Comprehending speech
Listening
Naming
Balance
Heartbeat and breathing
Spinal cord

The brain has three main parts: the cerebrum (top), where thinking takes place; the cerebellum (back) which deals with movement and balance; the brain stem (all the rest) which joins with the spinal cord.

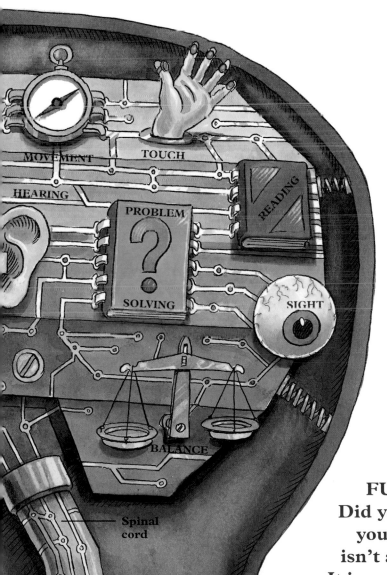

MOVEMENT
TOUCH
HEARING
READING
PROBLEM ? SOLVING
SIGHT
BALANCE
Spinal cord

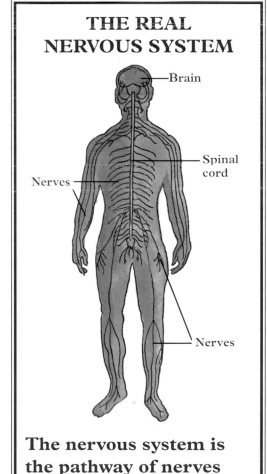

THE REAL NERVOUS SYSTEM

Brain
Spinal cord
Nerves
Nerves

The nervous system is the pathway of nerves that run throughout your body carrying messages.

FUNNY BONE
Did you know that your funny bone isn't a bone at all? It is a nerve in your elbow. That's why you get a sharp, shooting pain when you bash it.

ALL ABOUT THE SENSES

How do you keep track of the world around you? By using your five senses, that's how! Your eyes see, your nose smells, your skin feels, your ears hear and your tongue tastes. Each sense receiver is connected by nerves to your amazing brain.

You feel things with your skin. It tells you if things are hot or cold, rough or smooth. Your skin also feels pain. This warns your body of danger.

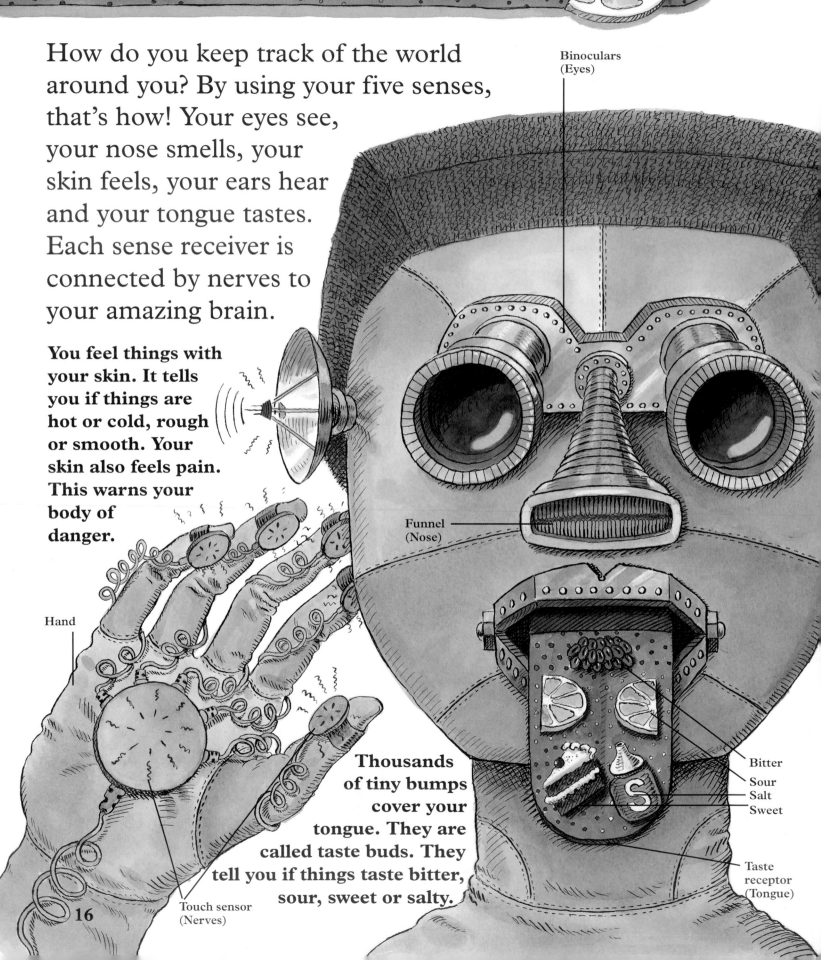

Binoculars (Eyes)

Funnel (Nose)

Hand

Thousands of tiny bumps cover your tongue. They are called taste buds. They tell you if things taste bitter, sour, sweet or salty.

Bitter

Sour

Salt

Sweet

Taste receptor (Tongue)

Touch sensor (Nerves)

TASTE AND SMELL

Have you noticed how horrible food tastes when you've got a cold? When you can't smell your food very well, you can't taste it very well either, because taste and smell work together.

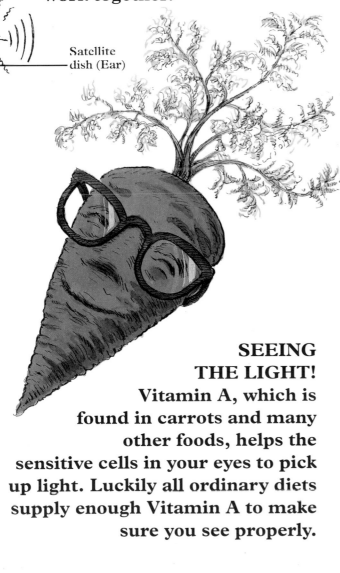

Satellite dish (Ear)

SEEING THE LIGHT!

Vitamin A, which is found in carrots and many other foods, helps the sensitive cells in your eyes to pick up light. Luckily all ordinary diets supply enough Vitamin A to make sure you see properly.

THE REAL SENSES

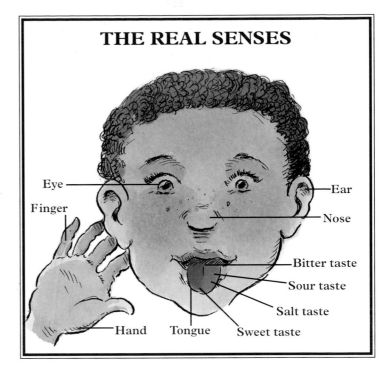

Eye
Finger
Ear
Nose
Bitter taste
Sour taste
Salt taste
Hand   Tongue   Sweet taste

THE EAR

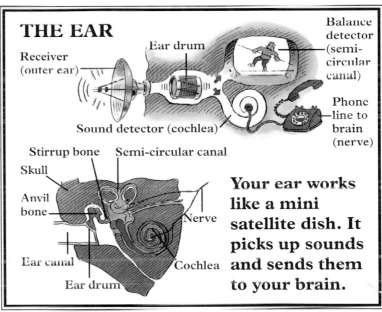

Receiver (outer ear)
Ear drum
Balance detector (semi-circular canal)
Sound detector (cochlea)
Phone line to brain (nerve)
Stirrup bone   Semi-circular canal
Skull
Anvil bone
Nerve
Ear canal
Cochlea
Ear drum

Your ear works like a mini satellite dish. It picks up sounds and sends them to your brain.

THE EYE

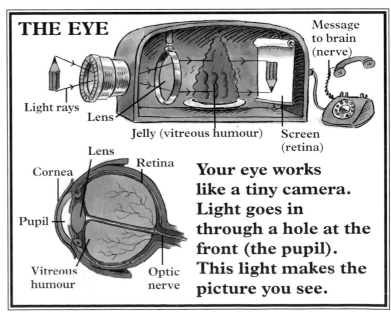

Message to brain (nerve)
Light rays
Lens
Jelly (vitreous humour)   Screen (retina)
Lens
Retina
Cornea
Pupil
Vitreous humour
Optic nerve

Your eye works like a tiny camera. Light goes in through a hole at the front (the pupil). This light makes the picture you see.

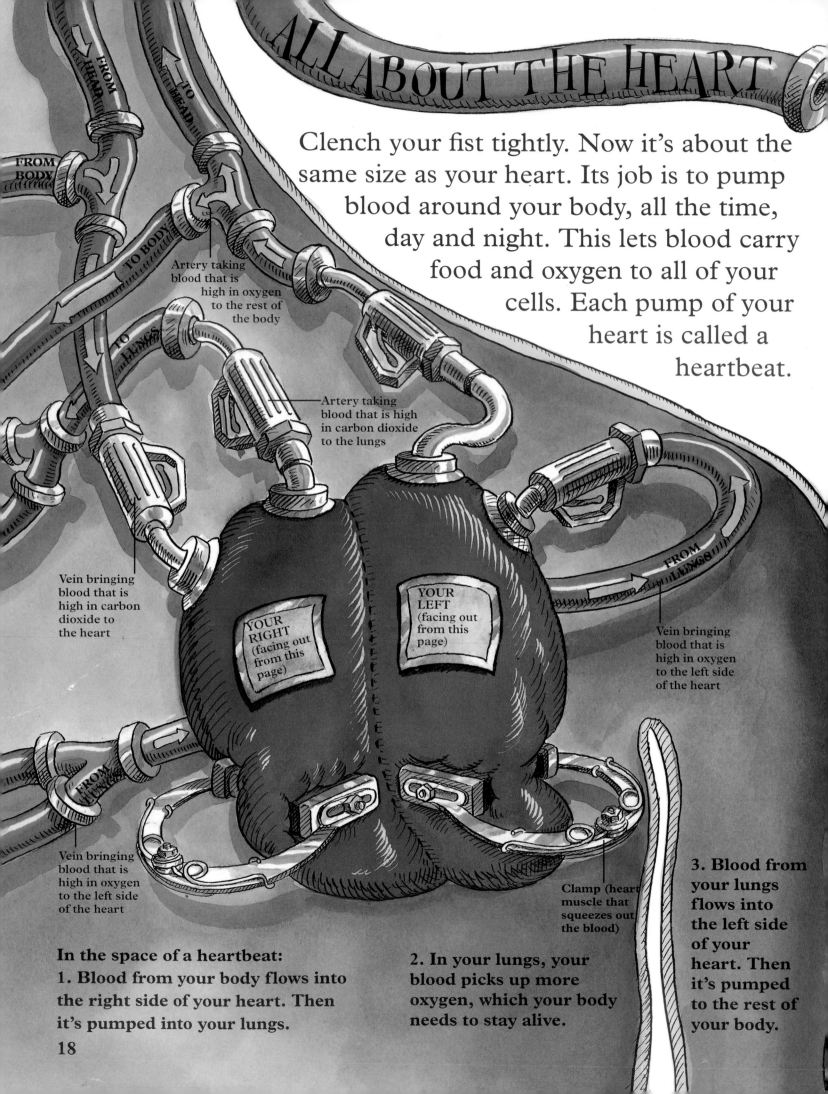

Clench your fist tightly. Now it's about the same size as your heart. Its job is to pump blood around your body, all the time, day and night. This lets blood carry food and oxygen to all of your cells. Each pump of your heart is called a heartbeat.

FROM HEAD

TO HEAD

FROM BODY

TO BODY

TO LUNGS

Artery taking blood that is high in oxygen to the rest of the body

Artery taking blood that is high in carbon dioxide to the lungs

FROM LUNGS

Vein bringing blood that is high in carbon dioxide to the heart

YOUR RIGHT (facing out from this page)

YOUR LEFT (facing out from this page)

Vein bringing blood that is high in oxygen to the left side of the heart

FROM LUNGS

Vein bringing blood that is high in oxygen to the left side of the heart

Clamp (heart muscle that squeezes out the blood)

In the space of a heartbeat:
1. Blood from your body flows into the right side of your heart. Then it's pumped into your lungs.

2. In your lungs, your blood picks up more oxygen, which your body needs to stay alive.

3. Blood from your lungs flows into the left side of your heart. Then it's pumped to the rest of your body.

18

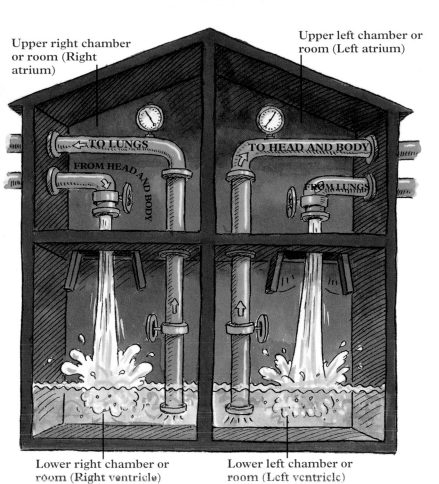

Upper right chamber or room (Right atrium)

Upper left chamber or room (Left atrium)

TO LUNGS

FROM HEAD AND BODY

TO HEAD AND BODY

FROM LUNGS

Lower right chamber or room (Right ventricle)

Lower left chamber or room (Left ventricle)

INSIDE YOUR HEART
Your heart is divided into four chambers, with walls of muscle in between. Thick tubes (pipes) connect the two top chambers with the two chambers below.

WHERE IS YOUR HEART?
Your heart sits in the middle of your chest, slightly to the left, between your two lungs. It's made of strong muscle.

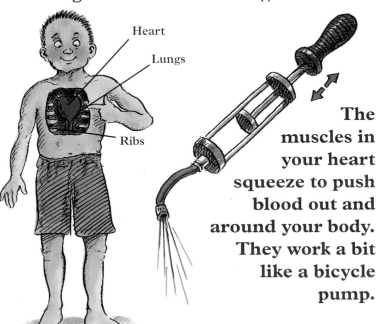

Heart

Lungs

Ribs

The muscles in your heart squeeze to push blood out and around your body. They work a bit like a bicycle pump.

Hearts are often linked with love. People used to think you felt things with your heart, not with your brain.

Did you know that your heart beats about 100,000 times a day? That's about 60 times a minute.

THE REAL HEART

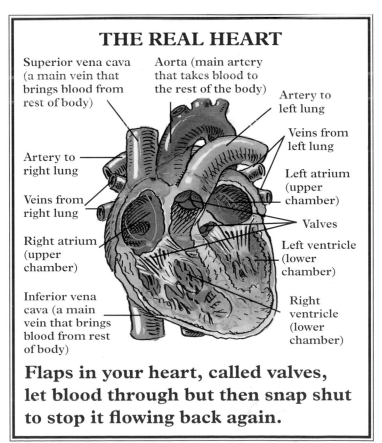

Superior vena cava (a main vein that brings blood from rest of body)

Aorta (main artery that takes blood to the rest of the body)

Artery to left lung

Veins from left lung

Artery to right lung

Left atrium (upper chamber)

Veins from right lung

Valves

Right atrium (upper chamber)

Left ventricle (lower chamber)

Inferior vena cava (a main vein that brings blood from rest of body)

Right ventricle (lower chamber)

Flaps in your heart, called valves, let blood through but then snap shut to stop it flowing back again.

ALL ABOUT BLOOD

What's the red stuff that seeps out if you cut yourself? Your blood! You need it to stay alive. Blood carries oxygen from the air you breathe, and useful bits from the food you eat, to every part of you. It also picks up and carries wastes to organs in the body that get rid of them.

WASTE

RED CELLS

Together, your heart and blood make up your circulatory system. "Circulatory" means going round and round. It takes about a minute for a blood cell to travel from the heart and back to it.

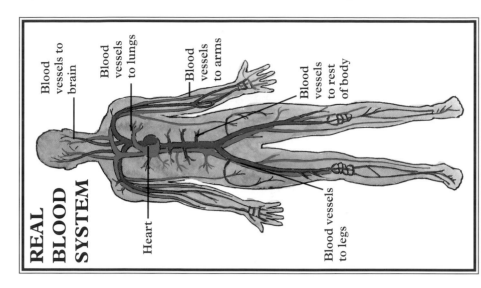

REAL BLOOD SYSTEM

Blood vessels to brain

Blood vessels to lungs

Blood vessels to arms

Blood vessels to rest of body

Heart

Blood vessels to legs

Blood flows around your body through tiny tubes. They're like tunnels on the underground, carrying trainloads of oxygen and food to nourish your body.

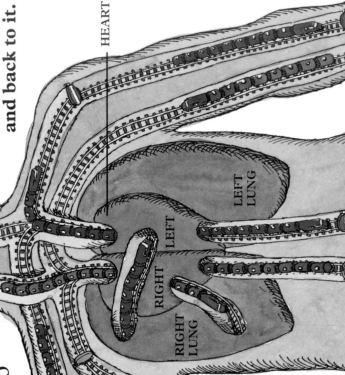

HEART

RIGHT LEFT

LEFT LUNG

RIGHT LUNG

If all the blood tubes in your body were put end to end, they'd go around the Earth two and a half times!

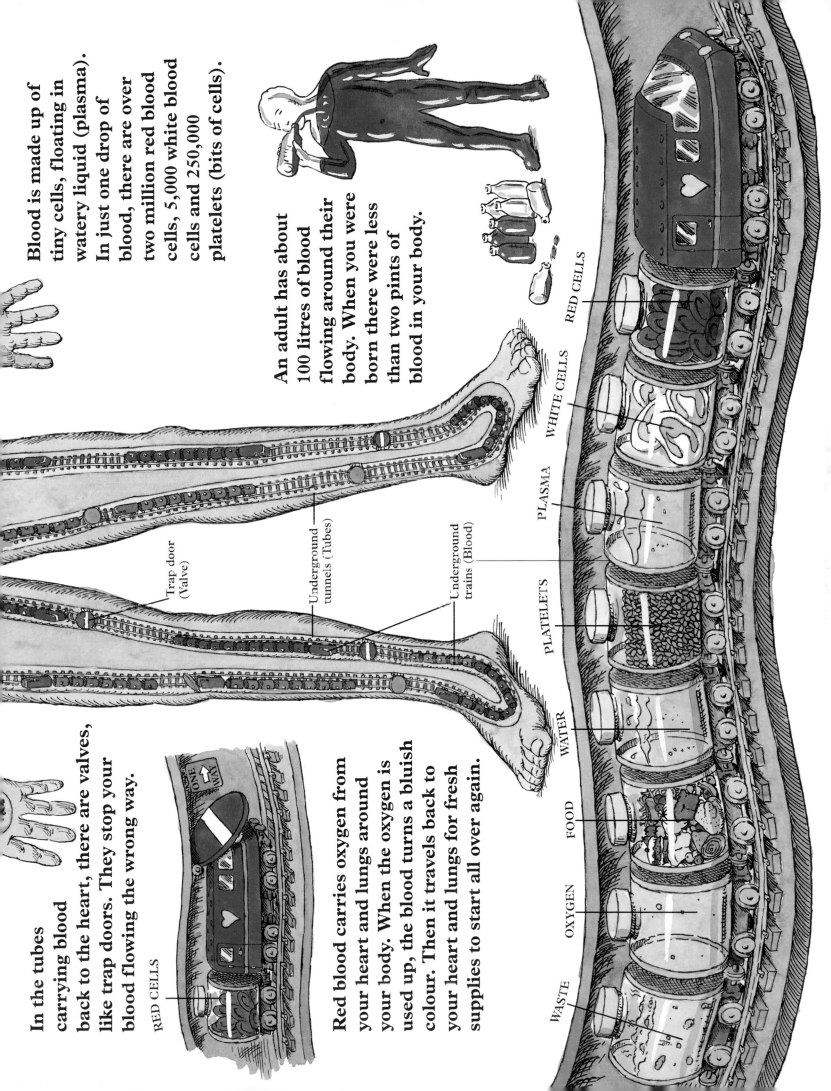

Blood is made up of tiny cells, floating in watery liquid (plasma). In just one drop of blood, there are over two million red blood cells, 5,000 white blood cells and 250,000 platelets (bits of cells).

An adult has about 100 litres of blood flowing around their body. When you were born there were less than two pints of blood in your body.

In the tubes carrying blood back to the heart, there are valves, like trap doors. They stop your blood flowing the wrong way.

RED CELLS

Red blood carries oxygen from your heart and lungs around your body. When the oxygen is used up, the blood turns a bluish colour. Then it travels back to your heart and lungs for fresh supplies to start all over again.

Trap door (Valve)

Underground tunnels (Tubes)

Underground trains (Blood)

RED CELLS

WHITE CELLS

PLASMA

PLATELETS

WATER

FOOD

OXYGEN

WASTE

You probably take breathing for granted. But you breathe all the time, without having to think. It's automatic. Your cells need a gas called oxygen to make them work. You get this from the air you breathe in. Your cells use this oxygen to get energy from the food you eat. As they do this, they make a waste gas, called carbon dioxide. This is the stale air that you breathe out. The main parts of your body used for breathing are your two lungs.

Fully grown lungs can hold an amazing nine pints of air.

When you breathe in, your lungs expand and draw in air. Your ribs move out to make space for the expanded lungs.

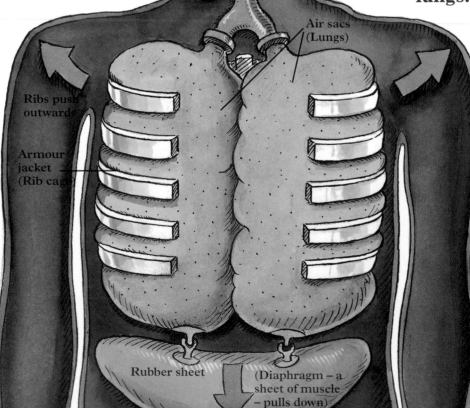

AIR IN

Air intake pipe (Wind pipe)

Guitar strings (Vocal cords)

Air sacs (Lungs)

Ribs push outwards

Armour jacket (Rib cage)

Rubber sheet

(Diaphragm – a sheet of muscle – pulls down)

SPEAK UP!

Your vocal cords are two thin strings stretched across your throat. When you speak, air flows across them and makes them wobble. This makes the sound of your voice.

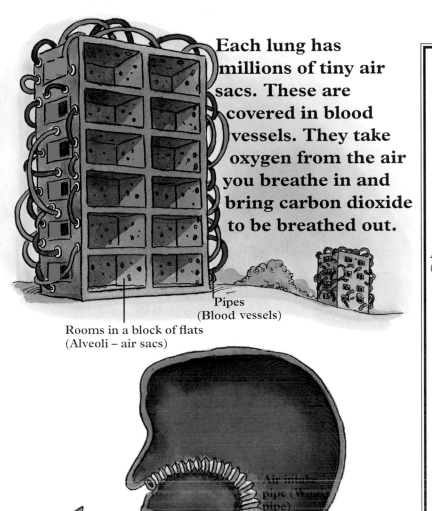

Each lung has millions of tiny air sacs. These are covered in blood vessels. They take oxygen from the air you breathe in and bring carbon dioxide to be breathed out.

Pipes (Blood vessels)

Rooms in a block of flats (Alveoli – air sacs)

THE REAL LUNGS

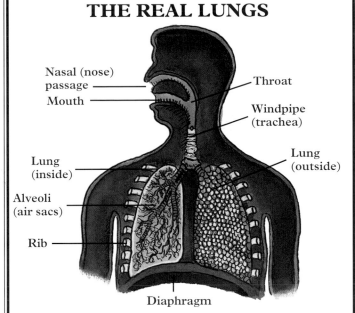

Nasal (nose) passage
Mouth
Throat
Windpipe (trachea)
Lung (inside)
Lung (outside)
Alveoli (air sacs)
Rib
Diaphragm

Your lungs are like spongy bags in your chest. Together with your mouth, nose and throat, they make up your body's respiratory system. "Respiratory" means the same as breathing.

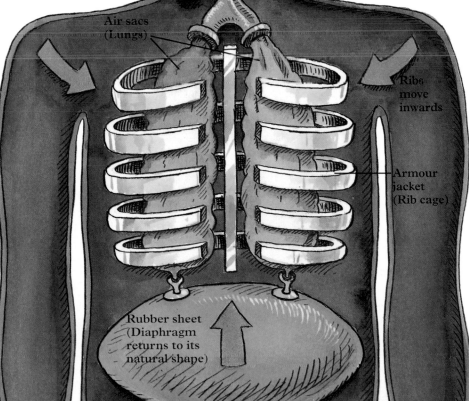

AIR OUT

Air intake pipe (Windpipe)

Guitar strings (Vocal cords)

Air sacs (Lungs)

Ribs move inwards

Armour jacket (Rib cage)

Rubber sheet (Diaphragm returns to its natural shape)

When you breathe out, your ribs push down and air is squeezed out of your lungs and up through your throat. Your diaphragm moves upwards.

Hic! Hic! Do you ever get hiccups? Hic! They happen if your diaphragm twitches sharply and your vocal cords snap shut with a loud noise. Drinking out of the wrong side of a glass is just one of the cures you can try.

23

All About Eating a Meal

Feeling hungry? That's your brain's way of telling you that your energy supplies are running low. Everything you do uses energy – even sleeping! Energy comes from food.

First, food has to be broken down into tiny pieces which are absorbed into the blood. Your blood then carries the goodness from the food to your cells.

THE REAL DIGESTIVE SYSTEM

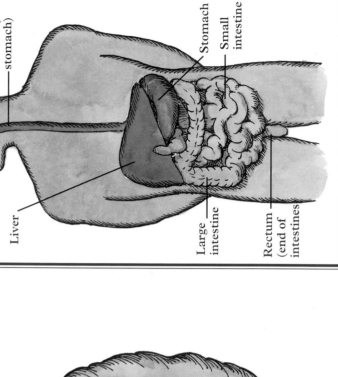

Throat

Oesophagus (pipe that leads to your stomach)

Mouth

Teeth

Liver

Stomach

Small intestine

Large intestine

Rectum (end of intestines)

Next step . . . swallowing! When you swallow, the food slips down a long tube in your throat and into your stomach. Gulp!

Saliva (A chemical juice that begins to break down the food and makes it slippery)

Food pipe (Oesophagus – tube that leads to your stomach)

Heart

Knives and forks (Teeth)

REAL TEETH

Skull

Jaw bone

Eye socket

Nose

2 pairs of canine teeth

4 pairs of incisor teeth

4 pairs of premolar teeth

6 pairs of molar teeth

In your mouth, your teeth chop and chew your food. A coating of watery spit (saliva) makes it slippery and easy to swallow.

In your stomach, the food is mashed and mushed into a slimy soup. Special juices help to dissolve it. Your stomach is made of strong muscle. It stretches as it fills with food. Then the soup trickles down into another long tube.

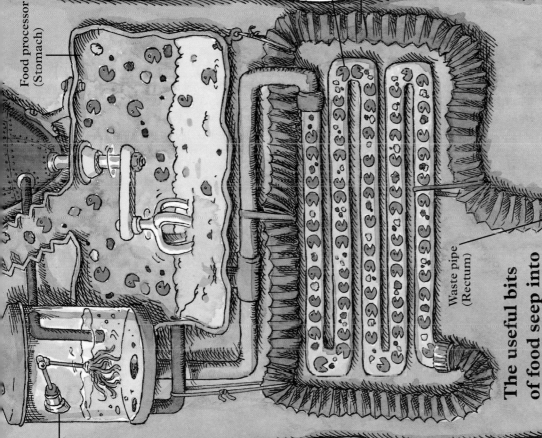

Food processor (Stomach)

Waste bin (Liver)

Pipe (Small intestine)

Pipe (Large intestine – about one and a half metres in length)

Waste pipe (Rectum)

The sides of the intestine tubes are made of strong muscles. They squeeze to push the food along them. It's a bit like squeezing toothpaste out a tube when you clean your teeth.

Before it goes to your cells, your blood carries the food to your liver. It helps get rid of any poisonous bits that might make you ill.

The useful bits of food seep into your blood from the small intestine. The blood carries them all over your body to your cells. Any waste food goes on into your large intestine.

Your small intestine is not actually small. It is a narrow tube that is between about five and eight metres long. It is coiled up tightly inside of you.

On average it takes a meal about three days to travel right through you.

ALL ABOUT WASTE

Some bits of food cannot be used. If they stayed in your body, they'd poison your cells and make you ill. So your body gets rid of them as waste. When you go to the toilet for a wee, you get rid of waste water and any dirty bits from your blood. When you go for a poo, you get rid of waste food.

Feeling sick? That's your body's way of getting rid of food that's bad or off. Otherwise it would poison your body. But you might also be sick if you've eaten too much!

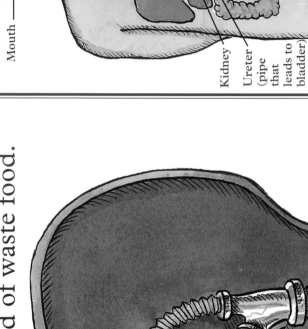

Heart

Liver

Stomach

Kidney

Small intestine

Rectum (end of intestine)

Large intestine

Anus (opening at end of intestine)

Bladder

Ureter (pipe that leads to bladder)

Kidney

Mouth

Your waste and digestive (eating) systems work together to get rid of wastes from your body. Here's what your waste system looks like.

Heart

Waste bin (Liver)

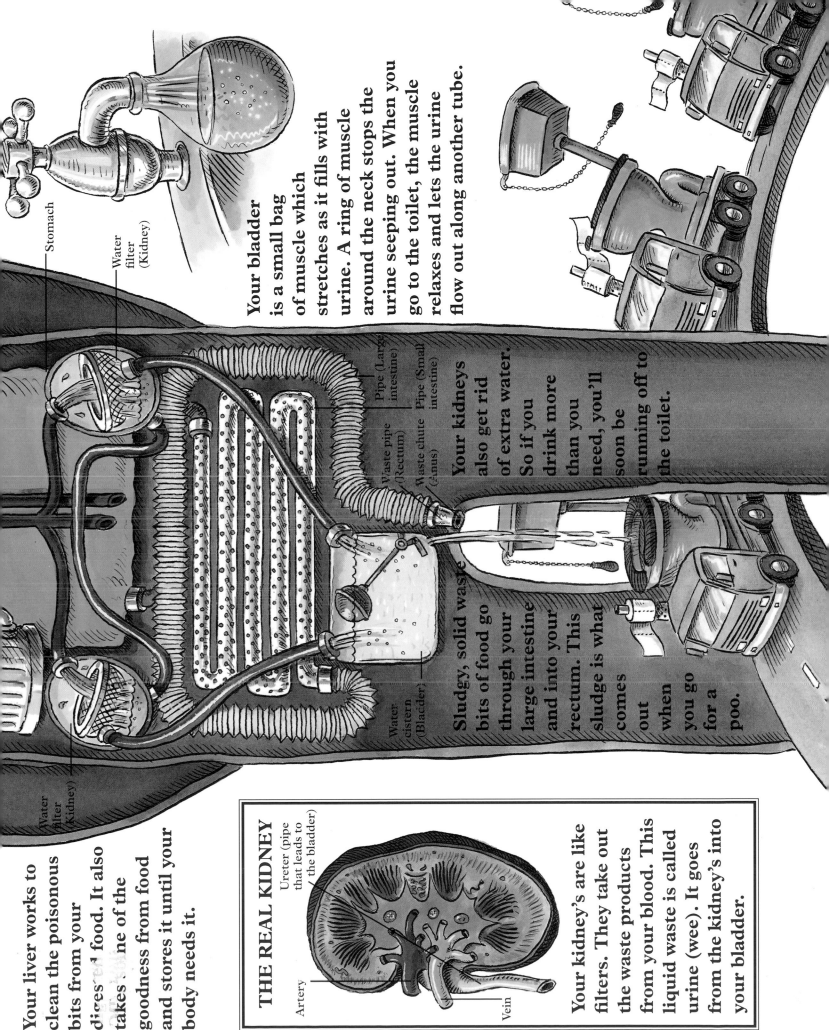

Your liver works to clean the poisonous bits from your digested food. It also takes some of the goodness from food and stores it until your body needs it.

Stomach

Water filter (Kidney)

Water filter (Kidney)

Your bladder is a small bag of muscle which stretches as it fills with urine. A ring of muscle around the neck stops the urine seeping out. When you go to the toilet, the muscle relaxes and lets the urine flow out along another tube.

Pipe (Large intestine)

Waste pipe (Rectum)

Pipe (Small intestine)

Waste chute (Anus)

Water cistern (Bladder)

Your kidneys also get rid of extra water. So if you drink more than you need, you'll soon be running off to the toilet.

Sludgy, solid waste bits of food go through your large intestine and into your rectum. This sludge is what comes out when you go for a poo.

THE REAL KIDNEY

Ureter (pipe that leads to the bladder)

Artery

Vein

Your kidney's are like filters. They take out the waste products from your blood. This liquid waste is called urine (wee). It goes from the kidney's into your bladder.

27

AMAZING BODY FACTS

Welcome to the amazing world of the human body and some astonishing facts about it. Did you know for example, that you become slightly taller in your sleep because you are lying down? But you shrink again when you get up.

What colour are these apples? About one in twenty people are red-green colour blind. This means that they can't tell the difference between red and green.

A man from India called Shridhar Chillal grew the longest fingernails in the world. Each nail on his left hand measured almost one metre.

In your lifetime, you will eat and digest about 30 tonnes of food.

Are you double-jointed? This doesn't mean you've got extra joints but that your ligaments are extra stretchy.

The aorta is the body's biggest artery. It's nearly 2.5 centimetres wide – that's wider than your thumb.

Aorta
2.5 cm
wide

The first heart transplant took place in 1967. Today surgeons can give people new lungs, kidneys, livers, skin and blood.

In your lifetime you pass about 40,000 litres of urine. That's around 500 baths full!

Different people have different types of blood, called A, B, O or AB.

Some cells live longer than others. Your brain cells have to last a lifetime. But red blood cells only live for four months.

Your skin is thinnest on your eyelids (half a millimetre), and thickest on the soles of your feet (five millimetres or more).

HAPPY
BIRTHDAY
Bone Cells
30 YEARS
Taste Cells
7 DAYS
Skin Cells
3 WEEKS

The strongest muscles are on each side of your mouth. You use them to bite with.

The sartorius is the longest muscle. It runs from your hip down to just below your knee. Its name comes from the Latin for "tailor" because tailors sat cross-legged to sew.

27

INDEX

air 22, 23
anus 26, 27
arteries 18, 19
    aorta 19, 29

bladder 26, 27
blood 6, 7, 13, 18,
    19, 20–21, 24,
    25, 29
bones 6, 7, 10, 11, 12,
    13, 17
brain 7, 10, 12,
    14–15, 16, 17, 24
breathing 7, 22, 23

carbon dioxide 18,
    22, 23
cells 6, 7, 8, 18, 22,
    24, 25, 29
    blood cells 21
    membrane 6
    nucleus 6
circulatory system 20

diaphragm 22, 23
digestion 7, 26, 28
digestive system 26

ears 7, 11, 13, 16, 17
eating 24–25, 28
eyes 7, 12, 16, 17,
    28, 29

food 7, 12, 13, 18,
    20, 21, 22, 24, 25,
    26, 27

hair 7, 8–9
    follicle 8, 9
heart 6, 7, 10, 12,
    18-19, 20, 21, 29
    chambers 19

intestines
    large 7, 24, 25,
    26, 27
    small 7, 24, 25,
    26, 27

joint 10, 11, 28

kidneys 7, 26, 27
    ureter 26, 27
knee 10, 11

ligament 10, 28
liver 7, 24, 25, 26, 27
lungs 7, 10, 18, 19,
    20, 21, 22–23
    alveoli 23

muscles 6, 7, 10,
    12–13, 19, 29
    biceps 12, 13
    sartorius 29
    triceps 12, 13

nails 7, 8, 9, 28
nerves 7, 14, 15,
    16, 17
nervous system 15
nose 7, 10, 16, 17

oesophagus 24
oxygen 13, 18, 20,
    21, 22, 23

rectum 24, 25, 26, 27
respiratory system 23
ribs 10, 22, 23

saliva 24
sebaceous gland 8, 9
senses 16–17
skeleton 6, 10–11
skin 7–8, 13, 16, 29
    dermis 8, 9
    epidermis 8, 9
    pore 9
skull 10
sleep 14, 28
smell 16, 17
spinal cord 15
stomach 7, 24, 25,
    26, 27
sweat gland 8, 9

taste 16, 17
taste buds 16
teeth 7, 24
tendons 13
tongue 16, 17
touch 8

urine 26, 27, 29

valves 19, 21
veins 18, 19
    inferior vena cava
    19
    superior vena cava
    19
vocal cords 22, 23

waste 7, 21, 26–27
wind pipe 22, 23